EVERYONE'S
Mandala
Coloring Book

By Monique Mandali

By the same author:
Everyone's Mandala Coloring Book (Volume 2)
Everyone's Mandala Coloring Book (Volume 3)

First printing, May 1978
Second printing, November 1978
Third printing, August 1991
Eighth printing, June 1996
Ninth printing, August 1997

ISBN 1-56044-014-7

Printed in Canada

Published by MANDALI PUBLISHING
P.O. Box 21852, Billings, Montana 59104
(1-800-347-1223), in cooperation with SkyHouse Publishers,
an imprint of Falcon®Publishing Co., Inc., Helena, Montana.

Design, typesetting, and other prepress work by
SkyHouse Publishers.

Distributed by Falcon Publishing Co., Inc.
P.O. Box 1718, Helena, Montana 59624
or call 1-800-582-2665.
Also distributed by
Bookpeople, New Leaf, Moving Books,
Baker & Taylor, and Ingram.

Visit our website at http://www.mandali.com.

Preface

THE WORD MANDALA is Sanskrit and literally means *center* and *circle*. It conveys the notion that any center is tied to its circumference and any circumference is always determined by its center. Together, they represent wholeness. The center and periphery appear separate, yet one does not exist without the other.

The center of each mandala symbolizes that which is beyond our linear concepts of time and space: the eternal *now* that is constant, yet always dynamic. The mandala's circumference, on the other hand, reflects its potential as well as boundaries.

Examples of mandalas abound in nature. Every cell in our body, for instance, is a living mandala. So is the iris of our eye, a snow crystal, a bird's nest, a bicycle wheel, and Planet Earth herself. The sun is the center of its own cosmic mandala. On a larger scale, I speculate that billions of galaxies in the universe somehow dance with each other in an incredible mandala choreography of which the center is eternity itself and in which each of us plays a role.

Mandalas are also reflected in the design of shelters such as Native American tipis, Inuit igloos, and Afghan yurts. Old European towns with a church and market place at their center from which cobbled streets fan outward to a protective wall are classic mandalas. So are, on a different level but of equal significance, the dynamics in everyday relationships between parent and child, teacher and student, master and apprentice, elder and youngster. In our own unique way, each of us is the center of a self-supporting, self-created mandala.

AS AN ART FORM mandalas have been known to all cultures throughout history. Individual designs vary greatly but they always have the following characteristics: a center, cardinal points that can be contained in a circle, and some form of symmetry. They can be very simple or extremely complex as in ancient Tibetan religious designs, Navajo sand paintings, and huge stained glass windows in medieval cathedrals. Traditionally, mandalas have been used by spiritual leaders, shamans, and healers as a source of wisdom, a form of meditation, and to reflect universal consciousness.

PSYCHOLOGICALLY mandalas represent the totality of our being or Self. The eminent Swiss psychoanalyst Carl G. Jung believed that they are our "eternal mind's eternal recreation," the path to our center, the voice of our unconscious, and the mirror of our becoming whole.

Because they reflect the human psyche, each of us responds instinctively to mandalas regardless of age, ethnic background, culture, or gender. Drawing and coloring mandalas is akin to undertaking a journey to the center of our being and shedding light onto something that was previously dark, hidden, and mysterious. It is a form of meditation which brings to our awareness messages from the unconscious, like bubbles that have been trapped at the bottom of the lake and are finally released.

As an activity, coloring mandalas can help us become more focused when we feel scattered and more peaceful when we are struggling with personal issues. Used in classrooms, they often calm hyperactive children and creatively engage others who are bored.

WHEN COLORING THESE MANDALAS children intuitively know what to do: they easily choose a design they like and the colors they want to use.

By the time we are adults, most of us have lost this spontaneity and often ask: what should I do? My answer is to forget your "shoulds." Find a quiet time and a calm space somewhere; take a few deep breaths and center yourself.

Next, leaf through the book and be aware of your feelings at the sight of each mandala. You'll notice that you feel attracted to some of the designs and that you dislike others. Let your intuition guide you and choose the design that appeals to you the most at the moment. Tear it out of the book along the perforated line and surround yourself with a rainbow of coloring crayons or pencils, water colors or magic markers.

Pick up the color that you are drawn to the most and *feel* what part of the mandala you would like to fill in. Proceed with other colors until you *feel* done, which means that there may be blank spaces left. You may wish to change or add to the design. When you are done, tape the mandala up on the wall, the refrigerator door, a dresser or bathroom mirror. Live with it, reflect on it. Let yourself be aware of feelings, thoughts, or memories.

Repeat this process with as many mandalas as you wish. Soon you may wish to draw your own. Most of all, *have fun.*

Monique Mandali, M.A., was born and raised in Belgium and is currently a wholistic therapist in Billings, Montana. She has been attracted to mandalas since childhood and drew these designs over a period of ten days while living in a tent one very snowy and cold Montana winter.